Fire from a Flint

'Enfolded in love' series
General Editor: Robert Llewelyn

FIRE FROM A FLINT

Daily Readings with William Law

Edited by
Robert Llewelyn and Edward Moss
Illustrated by Irene Ogden

Darton, Longman and Todd
London

First published in 1986 by
Darton, Longman and Todd Ltd
89 Lillie Road, London SW6 1UD

© 1986 The Julian Shrine and Edward Moss

ISBN 0 232 51696 0 ✓

British Library Cataloguing in Publication Data

Law, William
  Fire from a flint: daily readings with
  William Law.
  1. Devotional calendars
  I. Title II. Llewelyn, Robert III. Moss,
  Edward
  242'.2   BV4810

  ISBN 0–232–51696–0

Phototypeset by Input Typesetting Ltd,
London SW19 8DR
Printed and bound in Great Britain by
Anchor Brendon Ltd, Tiptree, Essex

Contents

Preface

It was my co-editor, Edward Moss, who suggested that the writings of William Law be included in this series. I had hoped this would be possible, but had felt insufficiently acquainted with Law's work to attempt the selection of readings myself. With an authority at hand the proposal was not to be refused.

Fifty and more years ago I read Law's best known book, *A Serious Call to a Devout and Holy Life*. It made a considerable impact at the time, and I admired, as we must all do, Law's facility and skill as a writer. But great though its influence has been on earlier generations, its severely moralistic tone must drastically limit its acceptance today. It is not a twentieth-century book for, with the advent of modern psychology, we have learnt much that is new of the springs of human behaviour. Some years on, however, Law underwent what he calls a second conversion, and his latter-day writings are on a different plane. It is on these that the following pages draw.

William Law (in his later books) stands almost alone among Christian writers of earlier times in declaring unequivocally the wrath-free nature of the love of God. It was this which first underlay my recent attention to Law, and I believe that we have here an important insight which the Church needs to absorb into its theology today. Like his distinguished predecessor, Julian of Norwich, Law teaches that the wrath is in us and not in God. 'There is no wrath,' he writes, 'that stands between God and us but what is awakened in the dark fire of our own fallen nature; and to quench this wrath, and not his own, God gave his only begotten Son to be made man' (p. 8). There are a number of readings on the same theme in these pages.

Law is an immensely powerful writer and his long, sustained sentences are packed with treasure which may well be missed in a superficial reading. He is not easy in large doses and the device of the single page and short paragraph, which is the hallmark of the present series, makes him much more manageable for the general reader. Even so, almost every page needs to be taken meditatively and slowly if the reader is to make Law's rich thought truly his own.

ROBERT LLEWELYN

William Law's life and writings

William Law was born in 1686 in the village of King's Cliffe in Northamptonshire, the son of a grocer and chandler who was of some standing locally. In 1705 he went to Emmanuel College, Cambridge. He was elected a fellow in 1711 and ordained a deacon in the same year. A document which survives from Law's early Cambridge days is a set of rules for the conduct of his life, of which the first is: 'To fix it deep in my mind that I have but one business upon my hands: to seek for eternal happiness by doing the will of God'. This and the seventeen rules which follow spell out a pattern of dedication and self-discipline that remained characteristic of him throughout his life.

Law was a High-Churchman and a believer in the divine right of kings. When George I came to the throne, Law could not in conscience swear allegiance to the new King and abjure his loyalty to the House of Stuart. In consequence in 1716 he resigned his fellowship, knowing that, as a 'non-juror', he would thereafter be debarred from any university or church appointment. It was a painful decision and one which meant that he would lead the rest of his life in relative obscurity, despite the success of some of his writings.

We know little of what Law did between 1716 and the year 1723 when he went to live in Putney in the house of Mr Gibbon, a well-to-do merchant, as tutor to his son Edward, later to be the father of the great historian of the same name. Law seems to have been treated as a member of the family and was able to entertain his friends as he wished. He remained in Putney until the elder Mr Gibbon's death in 1737, and the historian in his autobiography recalls Law as 'a worthy and pious person who believed all that he professed and practised all that he enjoined'.

Law was ordained a priest by a non-juring bishop in 1727. During his years in Putney, in addition to several powerful contributions to the theological controversies of the time, he published in 1726 *A Treatise upon Christian Perfection* and in 1729 his most famous book *A Serious Call to a Devout and Holy Life*. This was one of the most influential books of the century, and one which had a considerable effect on John and Charles Wesley, who were for a time friends and, in some degree, disciples of Law.

In 1737 Law moved to London and in 1740 returned to King's Cliffe where he owned a house. In 1743 he was joined there by Edward Gibbon's sister Hester and by Mrs Hutcheson, the widow of a member of Parliament. Together they formed a pious household, living according to the principles of the *Serious Call* and giving away nine-tenths of their joint income. Law had founded a school for fourteen poor girls in King's Cliffe as long ago as 1727, and in 1743 Mrs Hutcheson founded a similar school for eighteen boys. They also took responsibility for four poor widows; and their generosity to people in need attracted the tramps and beggars of the district to such an extent that in 1753 the parishioners made a complaint about them to the Justice of the Peace. Household prayers and devotions were conducted several times a day. It was a quiet and simple life, but by no means one of total seclusion; Law's brother George lived in the village and William was on good terms with the family. He received visitors and conducted a considerable correspondence.

In these years a major change came over William Law. An acute and learned theologian, he had nevertheless already been described in his Cambridge days as a 'celebrated enthusiast'; he was always an emotionalist in faith and highly conscious of the dimension of mystery. He had become acquainted with Tauler and the four-teenth-century Rhineland mystics at Cambridge and was particularly influenced by the philosophy of Malebranche, a rationalist in the succession of Descartes but an orthodox churchman with a strain of devotional mysticism in his thought. He was well acquainted with others in the tradition of what he called the mystical divines, from Dionysius the Areopagite to St John of the Cross and his own near-contemporary Fénelon. The Law of the *Serious Call* cannot himself, in spite of certain affinities, be described as a mystical writer; but when he encountered about 1735 the works of the Silesian cobbler Jacob Boehme (1575–1624), called Behmen by Law and his contemporaries, the impact on his whole life was remarkable. Boehme provided him with a new symbolic language through which the narrow, severe intensity of his devotional nature was released into a new freedom of love, joy and praise. This new life was reflected not only in the development of his thought but also in a new flexibility and eloquence in his prose.

Boehme's influence can be seen already in *A Demonstration* of 1737 (a work directed against the Deists), *The Ground and Reasons of Christian Regeneration* of 1739 and two *Answers to Dr Trapp* of 1740; but after 1740 Law published nothing for nine years while he pursued his study of the difficult and voluminous writings of 'the illuminated Behmen', for which purpose he learnt the 'High Dutch' language. Then between 1749 and 1754 he published *The Spirit of Prayer* and *The Spirit of Love* – effectively a ingle work in four parts – together with *The Way to Divine Knowledge*, intended as an introduction to a new edition of the works of Boehme, but presented as a continuation of the dialogues of *The Spirit of Prayer*. These, with a collection of letters and the moving *Address to the Clergy*, both published in 1761, constitute the main body of Law's mystical writings, and it is almost exclusively from these books that the present selection is drawn.

Law's friend Dr John Byrom had written as early as 1729 that he 'was mightily out of fashion', and as he grew older Law found himself even less in tune with a rational, sceptical age. But he was still a friend and oracle to many people and the last years at King's Cliffe seem to have been passed in an atmosphere of devotion, simplicity, benevolence and good humour. Wesley had broken with Law in 1738 and in 1755 he published a sharp attack on the mystical writings; but Law, powerful controversialist though he was, did not reply and he discouraged his friends from doing so. He died in 1761 with the words of a hymn on his lips. Hester Gibbon recorded that on the day before his death 'he said he had such an opening of the divine life within him that the fire of divine love quite consumed him'.

LAW THE MAN

There was always something formidable about William Law, combined with something awkward and remote. The young don's passionate sincerity commanded respect even when his Jacobitism and non-juror principles led him into trouble with the authorities. In the earlier years there was perhaps a touch of arrogance about him. Henri Talon in his admirable short study* suggests that the character of Ouranius in the *Serious Call* is in part a self-portrait: when he 'first entered into Holy Orders he had a haughtiness in his temper, a great contempt and disregard for all foolish and unreasonable people; but he has prayed away this spirit . . .' It may be this element in his character which made him so effective a polemical writer. But Law was ever aware of the need to humble himself and he did indeed pray his haughtiness away – so much so that this man of great learning came to disparage learning and to attach greater importance to the religious instincts of unlettered people, like his character Rusticus, than to the views of theologians. It is still perhaps true that the relationships in which he was involved were seldom on a level of full equality. Even his lifelong friend and supporter John Byrom took a deferential attitude towards him. Psychologically,

* *William Law, A Study in Literary Craftsmanship*, Rockliff 1948.

it could be argued, the breach with John Wesley in 1738 was as much a breaking-away by the younger man from Law's quasi-parental authority as it was a dispute on points of theology. Talon is critical of this characteristic, and perhaps with justice; but it is one which grows out of the awkwardness and sometimes insensitivity of the introvert in developing close human relationships; and to no small extent it may be attributed to the isolation from the intellectual mainstream enforced by Law's status as a non-juror.

What is impressive about him, however, is the way in which he grows and changes. Law the stickler had been closely involved in controversies within the non-juring community about points of ritual and practice, but from early in the 1730s he lost interest in these matters. His theological sympathies, never narrow, grew into a remarkably broad ecumenism that stretched from the Quakers to the saints of the Counter-Reformation. His earlier moral teaching, very much a matter of determination and the rational will, developed under Boehme's influence into a noble doctrine of God's love and the 'process of Christ' within each individual human being. His last great work is fittingly called *The Spirit of Love*.

He still remained the same person, sometimes awkward, even rough, in his dealings, still strong in his certitudes, more a director than a listener, still eccentric in the extremity of some of his views; but with all this the Law of the King's Cliffe years was clearly a man of great humility and goodwill. We have glimpses of him playing with his nephew's children or troubled at the sight of a captive bird; and A K Walker in his biography* quotes the rector of a neighbouring village as saying that Law used to see company, was free in conversation and had a warm and loving heart and universal charity.

LAW'S MYSTICAL THEOLOGY

The strongest influence upon the intellectual climate of England in the early eighteenth century was the achievement of Isaac Newton, who seemed to have unlocked the heavens and reduced the universe to order and clarity with the key of human reason. Beyond this a great succession of philosophers from Descartes to Locke and Berkeley had brought a new kind of detached scientific rationalism to the understanding of both nature and man. The pressing task of theology was in some way to come to terms with this new understanding; and the most characteristic response was to move towards a Deism which enthroned reason as the test of truth, which saw God in the image of a divine clockmaker and which tended to dismiss much of the religion of earlier times as superstition.

In an important sense William Law's theology was also an attempt to come to terms with the intellectual climate of his age. But his response was very different. He attacked the Deists with a sarcastic force which made him one of the great controversialists of the time. And his starting-point was the recognition of mystery. He had a Pascalian sense of the grandeur and misery of the

* *William Law: His Life and Work*, SPCK 1973.

human condition. 'No revealed mysteries can more exceed the comprehension of man than the state of human life itself.' 'We must be surrounded with mystery.' 'Be no reasoners upon the mystery . . . to give yourself up to reasoning and notional conceptions is to turn from God and wander out of the way of all divine communication.' And he had a theory of knowledge to support this view. 'It is the sensibility of the soul that must receive what this world can communicate to it; it is the sensibility of the soul that must receive what God can communicate to it. Reason may follow after in either case, and view through its own glass what is done, but it can do no more.'

Yet he remained a man of his time; and this comes through in the moralistic works of his middle years. The *Serious Call* rests essentially on argument directed to convincing the rational mind, and this is no doubt why of all his works it had by far the widest appeal in his own time and for long afterwards; but it is also why its exhortations and character sketches, for all their cogency and sharp observation, do not speak with the same force to a post-Freudian generation. They do not penetrate sufficiently into the deeper emotional roots of human behaviour. But the encounter with Boehme, as we have already seen, was to act as the catalyst of a profound transformation in Law. Reason was, as it were, dethroned a second time. The later writings are often surprisingly modern in their psychology. Law becomes aware of the depths of what we would call the unconscious: 'Oh break open the gates of the great deep in my soul . . . ' He knows that a state of great distress can be the opening to a profound renewal: 'O happy famine which leaves you not so much as the husk of one human comfort to feed upon. For this is the time and place for all that good and life and salvation to happen to you which happened to the Prodigal Son.' And he is confident in the Holy Spirit who, in St Paul's words, 'speaks in the inner man': 'Above all let me tell you that the book of all books is your own heart, in which are written and engraven the deepest lessons of divine instruction; learn therefore to be deeply attentive to the presence of God in your hearts, who is always speaking, always instructing, always illuminating that heart that is attentive to him.'

The immense effect of Boehme's work upon Law implies that it met a need which had been long maturing. This seems to have been the need for a system of thought which could reconcile in one structure not only the truths of biblical revelation, but a rational account of the world of nature which was conformable to the science of the day and, not least, the psychological reality of the experience and process of Christian redemption as Law had come to know it. Above all it had to explain how the fact of evil in the world could be reconciled with the existence of a God of love.

Attempts have been made to find such a rational theodicy, to 'justify the ways of God to men' as Milton put it, ever since the time of Job, and no final answer in rational terms has ever been achieved. In every age, however, men have faced this problem anew, and Law found in Boehme the elements of an explanation which for him carried overwhelming conviction and set him free to proclaim without reservation the gospel that God is all love; that his righteousness and justice are themselves nothing but love; that there is no element of anger, wrath or retribution in him; and that he wills only good to all his creatures. This is the core of Law's teaching.

Talon remarks justly that the truths which Law reached in his thinking organized themselves into a myth of impressive grandeur and beauty. The word myth is well chosen (though it would not have been used by Law himself). A myth is not the same as the ttruth because the final truth of the ultimate things with which it is concerned is always beyond words and beyond images. But if it is a true myth it can be truth-bearing to one who responds to it creatively. Law's theodicy consists of two main elements, the one cosmological and the other psychological. The first element represents an elaboration of the very brief references in the Bible to the fall of the angels (e.g., 2 Peter 2:4), together with a variety of scientific speculations drawn partly from Newton but mainly from more ancient sources. Philosophically this is a sophisticated construction, but it can hardly speak directly to us now without reinterpretation, in an age when the literal truth of Genesis is no longer assumed and our scientific conceptions of matter and energy have greatly changed.

The second main element in Law's theodicy is concerned with the mind, heart and soul of man; and this still has great relevance today, all the more so because it is firmly and closely based on the teaching of the New Testament. God breathed into Adam, and so into the whole human race, the inspoken Word of Life, the seed of salvation, the spark of the divine nature which is Christ within us; and this gives each of us the capacity to be redeemed, to be born again into the life of paradise. To exercise this capacity we have to use the free will that has been given to us in order to turn away from self and turn towards God. God's love is always ready to meet us and make us one with him. But this at-one-ment is not any kind of purchase, it is the 'process' of Christ who is already within us, the 'inward essential growth' of the divine life from the seed which is present in every man, a process which in some sense recapitulates in each individual the birth, life, sufferings, death, resurrection and ascension of the Lord himself. 'Christ given for us is Christ given into us.' It is through our turning to God in prayer that this renewal is begun and continued within us. And correspondingly if we turn towards earthly things and direct our prayer to the creation rather than the creator, we move inexorably towards the condition of wrath, in separation from God. Heaven and hell both begin in this life.

Even though we can no longer share many of Law's historical and scientific assumptions, we are in no position to be patronizing or dismissive even about his cosmological speculations; Law was here facing up to questions which too often we evade, and to which we have no better answers than his. Every attempt to provide a framework of ultimate understanding reaches into final mysteries, and no one was more aware than Law himself of the ultimate inadequacy of human thoughts and words. Perhaps the closest modern equivalent to his great myth is the myth constructed by Teilhard de Chardin. Law wrote in a Newtonian, Teilhard in a Darwinian, context. Teilhard was much more the scientist, Law much more the poet. Yet each in his way was attempting to make some kind of total sense of the human condition and the divine drama of the cosmos. Teilhard may have thought of his work as fundamentally a scientific hypothesis (though many scientists would not accept it as such). Law, too, thought of his work as serious science, though perhaps even in his own day few would have agreed with him.

It is important, however, in Law's case to emphasize that his essential concern was never to explain the origin and fate of the world and its creatures; it was to preach the gospel. The framework of theodicy was necessary not for its own sake, but to enable him to articulate the Christian message in terms appropriate to his day. His books contain no succinct and systematic exposition of his ideas because his real concern was elsewhere. He is always the evangelist, always persuading, always aiming to reach the heart as well as the intellect, constantly breaking out into poetry and exhortation. As he wrote towards the end of his life:

As the Baptist said 'He must increase, but I must decrease', so every faithful teacher says of his doctrine, it must decrease and end as soon as it has led to the true teacher. All that I have written for nearly thirty years has been only to show that we have no master but Christ, nor can have any living divine knowledge but from his holy nature born and revealed in us. Not a word in favour of Jacob Behmen but because, above every writer in the world, he has made all that is found in the kingdom of grace and the kingdom of nature to be one continual demonstration that dying to self, to be born again of Christ, is the one only possible salvation of the sons of fallen Adam.

In his central stress on the goodness and love of God and his view that there is in God no wrath whatever, Law comes near to his great predecessor Julian of Norwich, though there is no evidence that he was acquainted with her writings. It is the same stress which led to his characteristic teaching about the atonement – 'that the innocent Christ did not suffer to quiet an angry Deity'; that 'Christ is in no other sense our full, perfect and sufficient atonement than as his nature and spirit are born and formed in us'. It led to his admirably ecumenical sympathies: 'He therefore that would like as God likes and condemn as God condemns must have neither the eyes of the Papist nor the Protestant; he must like no truth the less because Ignatius Loyola or John Bunyan were very zealous for it, nor have the less aversion to any error because Dr Trapp or George Fox [the Quaker] had brought it forth.' And there are indications that the logic of his stress on love brought him at the end of his life to the 'universalist' position that in the final fire of judgement all men and all things would be saved and hell itself would be redeemed.

Law had great sympathy for human sinners and the story of the Prodigal Son is one which recurs in his writing. But he was quite uncompromising in his demand for a total death to self, a total surrender to the will of God. In this he follows directly the teaching of the Sermon on the Mount and of all the New Testament writers. A Christian is not called to be moderately good; he is called to perfection. He is not required to patch up and improve his existing self; he is to put off the old man altogether and put on another self conformed to Christ. All this can seem discouraging; and in these days of psychological theories of self-fulfilment it may even be denounced as impossible and wrong. But it is not. The New Testament doctrine is sound and right, psychologically as well as morally. As Law argues, 'Christ must first come as a discoverer and reprover of sin'. Until we face the fact of our sin, we cannot begin to change and grow; but our very consciousness of sin, Law says, is evidence that Christ is there already within us; and we can take heart from the fact that 'he that discovers is the same Christ that takes away sin'. Law denounces our 'multiplicity of wills' as the essence of fallen nature. But in doing so he does not mean, absurdly, that we should cease to have any practical wishes or intentions in the world; rather, that all our separate wills should be subordinated to God's one will – just as we pray that they should in the Lord's Prayer. We can achieve this only through the spirit of prayer: 'Everything calls for it, everything is to be done in it and governed by it.' As humans we are constantly falling into sin, but through prayer we can be as constantly drawn back by the 'divine loadstone' towards our true perfection. Even though we may fully know such perfection only perhaps in rare moments of grace, we must always be facing towards the perfect life.

LAW AS A WRITER

William Law wrote in his younger days with force, astringency and a broadsword wit. In his later works his writing acquired a new variety of rhythm and imagery and a new intensity of feeling, without losing its cogency and vigour. There is hardly a weak sentence or paragraph to be found in these books. He is one of the masters of English prose. Yet it must be acknowledged that as works of art the later writings are by no means altogether successful. Law's art is that of rhetoric, the art of persuasion. He had strength of intellect, burning sincerity, and superb, even luxuriant eloquence. If he had only had a pulpit, he would surely have left us sermons to rival or outmatch those of Donne or Bossuet. But in the absence of such a discipline as that of the sermon form, his paragraphs are poured out like a flow of molten lava, glowing and continuous, but not always building up a coherent, larger whole.

It is not that Law's ideas are intellectually incoherent; they represent a much stronger system of thought than the casual reader may recognize, and one which is still highly relevant today. But his books show little evidence of larger-scale organization. He develops his thought by constantly circling round the same themes, saying the same thing again and again in different ways, with an endless originality of verbal resource, refining and elaborating as he goes. One result of this procedure is that these books gain in some respects by being presented in systematic anthology rather than as they stand.★ *The Spirit of Prayer* and *The Spirit of Love* are indeed not without explicit theme and structure; but Law is nevertheless constantly crossing and recrossing his own tracks. The device which he adopts of beginning these works with a major disquisition followed by a series of somewhat stilted dialogues serves only to add to the effect of repetitive improvisation, even though every time he returns to a theme he develops it in some new and striking way.

Law tends to develop his thought on several different levels – biblical, cosmological, psychological – simultaneously. This can add greatly to the poetic power and resonance of his work, but it can also lead to difficulties for some readers, especially those who are not familiar with the framework of Behmenist ideas – the myth as I have called it – which provides much of the rich language of symbols through which Law develops his themes. But such difficulties do not arise in relation to the short readings brought together in this book. Through the use of symbolic language

★ Cf. Alexander Whyte, *William Law, Non-Juror and Mystic*, Hodder and Stoughton 1893; and Stephen Hobhouse, *Selected Mystical Writings of William Law*, Rockliff 1938, revised edition 1948.

Law was enabled to achieve powerful communication about great mysteries – the human predicament, the fact of evil, the grace of God – which can by no means be reduced to simple rationality. For him there could be no profit in reading Boehme (or, presumably, his own work) in a pedantic, critical way 'under the guidance of our own Babylonian reason'. 'Words are but words; and though they be spoken even by the messengers of God, as angels or prophets or apostles, when they do their best they can only do as John the Baptist did, bear witness to the light: but the light itself, which can only give light to the soul, is God himself.' Law was indeed a witness to the light.

EDWARD MOSS

'I stand at the door and knock'

Neither Christ nor his benefits and blessings have the nature of things done, or gone and past, but are always present, always in being, always doing and never done.

'Jesus Christ, the same yesterday, today and for ever', always was, now is, and ever will be present as the Saviour of the world. He is the Alpha and Omega, the beginning and the end, and therefore equally present in and through all from the beginning to the end.

'Behold,' says he, 'I stand at the door and knock; if any man hear my voice and open the door, I will come in to him and will sup with him.' Thus he stood at the door of Adam's heart as near as he stood to the apostles'; and thus he stands, and will stand, knocking at the door of every man's heart until time shall be no more.

Love is my bait

Oh Humanus, love is my bait. You must be caught by it; it will put its hook into your heart and force you to know that of all strong things nothing is so strong, so irresistible as divine love. It brought forth all the creation; it kindles all the life of heaven, it is the song of all the angels of God. It has redeemed all the world; it seeks for every sinner upon earth; it embraces all the enemies of God; and from the beginning to the end of time the one work of providence is the one work of love.

Ask what God is? His name is love; he is the good, the perfection, the peace, the joy, the glory and blessing of every life. Ask what Christ is? He is the universal remedy of all evil broken forth in nature and creatures. He is the destruction of misery, sin, darkness, death and hell. He is the resurrection and life of all fallen nature. He is the unwearied compassion, the long-suffering pity, the never-ceasing mercifulness of God to every want and infirmity of human nature.

The spirit of love

All religion is the spirit of love; all its gifts and graces are the gifts and graces of love; it has no breath, no life, but the life of love.

Nothing exalts, nothing purifies but the fire of love; nothing changes death into life, earth into heaven, men into angels, but love alone.

Love breathes the spirit of God; its words and works are the inspiration of God. Love speaks not of itself, but the Word, the eternal Word of God speaks in it. All that love speaks, that God speaks, because love is God.

Love is heaven revealed in the soul; it is light and truth; it is infallible; it has no errors, for all errors are the wantof love.

Love has no more of pride than light has of darkness; it stands and bears all its fruits from a depth and root of humility.

Love is of no sect or party; it neither makes nor admits of any bounds; you may as easily enclose the light or shut up the air of the world in one place, as confine love to a sect or party. It lives in the liberty, the universality, the impartiality of heaven.

The healing power of love

Love, like the spirit of God, rides upon the wings of the wind, and is in union and communion with all the saints that are in heaven and on earth.

Love is quite pure; it has no by-ends; it seeks not its own; it has but one will, and that is to give itself into everything and overcome all evil with good.

Lastly, love is the Christ of God; it comes down from heaven; it regenerates the soul from above; it blots out all transgressions; it takes from death its sting, from the devil his power, and from the serpent his poison. It heals all the infirmities of our earthly birth; it gives eyes to the blind, ears to the deaf, and makes the dumb to speak; it cleanses the lepers and casts out devils, and puts man in paradise before he dies.

The discovery of ourselves

So far as we, by true resignation to God, die to the element of selfishness and our own will, so far as by universal love we die to envy, so far as by humility we die to pride, so far as by meekness we die to wrath, so far we get away from the devil, enter into another kingdom and leave him to dwell without us in his own elements.

The greatest good that any man can do to himself is to give leave to this inward deformity to show itself, and not to strive by any art or management, either of negligence or amusement, to conceal it from him.

First, because the root of a dark fire-life within us, which is of the nature of hell, with all its elements of selfishness, envy, pride and wrath, must be in some sort discovered to us, and felt by us, before we can enough feel and enough groan under the weight of our disorder.

Repentance is but a kind of table-talk until we see so much of the deformity of our inward nature as to be in some degree frightened and terrified at the sight of it.

There must be some kind of earthquake within us, something that must rend and shake us to the bottom, before we can be enough sensible either of the state of death we are in, or enough desirous of that Saviour who alone can raise us from it.

Hearsay-religion and true faith

The reason why we know so little of Jesus Christ as our Saviour, why we are so destitute of that faith in him which alone can change, rectify and redeem our souls, why we live starving in the coldness and deadness of a formal, historical hearsay-religion, is this: we are strangers to our own inward misery and wants, we know not that we lie in the jaws of death and hell.

We keep all things quiet within us, partly by outward forms and modes of religion and morality, and partly by the comforts, cares and delights of this world. Hence it is that we believe in a Saviour not because we feel an absolute want of one, but because we have been told there is one, and that it would be a rebellion against God to reject him.

True faith is a coming to Jesus Christ to be saved and delivered from a sinful nature, as the Canaanite woman came to him and would not be denied. It is a faith that in love and longing and hunger and thirst and full assurance will lay hold on Christ as its loving, assured, certain and infallible Saviour.

It is this faith that breaks off all the bars and chains of death and hell in the soul; it is to this faith that Christ always says what he said in the gospel: 'Your faith has saved you, your sins are forgiven you; go in peace.'

God's universal love

Some people have an idea of the Christian religion as if God was thereby declared so full of wrath against fallen man that nothing but the blood of his only begotten Son could satisfy his vengeance. These are miserable mistakers of the divine nature and miserable reproachers of his great love and goodness.

For God is love, yea all love; and so all love that nothing but love can come from him; and the Christian religion is nothing else but an open, full manifestation of his universal love towards all mankind.

As the light of the sun has only one common nature towards all objects that can receive it, so God has only one common nature of goodness towards all created nature, breaking forth in infinite flames of love upon every part of creation and calling everything to the highest happiness it is capable of.

God so loved man, when his fall was foreseen, that he chose him to salvation in Christ Jesus before the foundation of the world. When man was actually fallen, God was so without all wrath towards him that he sent his only begotten Son into the world to redeem him. Therefore God has no nature towards man but love, and all that he does to man is love.

The wrath is in us and not in God

There is no wrath that stands between God and us but what is awakened in the dark fire of our own fallen nature; and to quench this wrath, and not his own, God gave his only begotten Son to be made man.

God has no more wrath in himself now than he had before the creation, when he had only himself to love. The precious blood of his Son was not poured out to pacify himself (who in himself had no nature towards man but love), but it was poured out to quench the wrath and fire of the fallen soul, and to kindle in it a birth of light and love.

As man lives and moves and has his being in the divine nature, and is supported by it, whether his nature be good or bad, so the wrath of man, which was awakened in the dark fire of his fallen nature, may, in a certain sense, be called the wrath of God, as hell itself may be said to be in God because nothing can be out of his immensity. Yet this hell is not God, but the dark habitation of the devil. And this wrath which may be called the wrath of God is not God, but the fiery wrath of the fallen soul.

God's will is the only good

The soul is only so far cleansed from its corruption, so far delivered from the power of sin, and so far purified, as it has renounced all its own will and own desire to have nothing, receive nothing and be nothing but what the one will of God chooses for it and does to it.

This and this alone is the true Kingdom of God opened in the soul when stripped of all selfishness, it has only one love and one will in it when it has no motion or desire but what branches from the love of God and resigns itself wholly to the will of God.

There is nothing evil or the cause of evil to either man or devil but his own will; there is nothing good in itself but the will of God.

He, therefore, who renounces his own will turns away from all evil; and he who gives himself up wholly to the will of God puts himself in the possession of all that is good.

The will of God and the harmony of creation

God created everything to partake of his own nature, to have some degree and share of his own life and happiness. Nothing can be good or evil, happy or unhappy, but as it does or does not stand in the same degree of divine life in which it was created, receiving in God and from God all that good that it is capable of, and co-operating with him according to the nature of its powers and perfections.

As soon as it turns to itself and would, as it were, have a sound of its own, it breaks off from the divine harmony and falls into the misery of its own discord; and all its workings then are only so many sorts of torment or ways of feeling its own poverty.

The redemption of mankind can then only be effected, the harmony of the creation can then only be restored when the will of God is the will of every creature.

For this reason our blessed Lord, having taken upon him a created nature, so continually declares against the doing of anything of himself and always appeals to the will of God as the only motive and end of everything he did, saying that it was his meat and drink to do the will of him that sent him.

The state of our will makes the state of our life

It is the state of our will that makes the state of our life; when we receive anything from God and do everything for God, everything does us the same good and helps us to the same degree of happiness.

Sickness and health, prosperity and adversity, bless and pacify such a soul in the same degree. As it turns everything towards God, so everything becomes divine to it. For he that seeks God in everything is sure to find God in everything.

When we thus live wholly unto God, God is wholly ours and we are happy in all that happiness of God. For in uniting with him in heart and will and spirit we are united to all that he is and has in himself.

This is the purity and perfection of life that we pray for in the Lord's Prayer, that God's Kingdom may come and his will be done in us as it is in heaven. And this, we may be sure, is not only necessary but attainable by us, or our Saviour would not have made it a part of our daily prayer.

The book of all books

The book of all books is in your own heart, in which are written and engraven the deepest lessons of divine instruction; learn therefore to be deeply attentive to the presence of God in your hearts, who is always speaking, always instructing, always illuminating that heart that is attentive to him.

Here you will meet the divine light in its proper place, in that depth of your souls, where the birth of the Son of God and the proceeding of the Holy Ghost are always ready to spring up in you.

And be assured of this, that so much as you have of inward love and adherence to his holy light and spirit within you, so much as you have of real unaffected humility and meekness, so much as you are dead to your own will and self-love, so much as you have of purity of heart, so much, and no more, nor any further, do you see and know the truths of God.

The prayer of the heart

 All outward power that we exercise in the things about us is but as a shadow in comparison of that inward power that resides in our will, imagination and desires. These communicate with eternity and kindle a life which always reaches either heaven or hell.

Our desire is not only thus powerful and productive of real effects, but it is always alive, always working and creating in us – I say creating, for it has no less power, it perpetually generates either life or death in us.

And here lies the ground of the great efficacy of prayer, which, when it is the prayer of the heart, the prayer of faith, has a kindling and creating power, and forms and transforms the soul into everything that its desires reach after.

It has the key to the kingdom of heaven and unlocks all its treasures, it opens, extends and moves that in us which has its being and motion in and with the divine nature, and so brings us into real union and communion with God.

What we mean by the heart

That which we mean by the heart plainly speaks thus much: that it is a kind of life and motion within us which everyone knows contains all that is good or bad in us; that we are that which our hearts are, let us talk and reason and dispute what we will about goodness and virtue; and that this state of our heart is as distinct from and independent of all speculations of our reasoning faculties as it is distinct from and independent of all the languages in which a scholar can reason and speculate about it.

For our heart is our manner of existence, or the state in which we feel ourselves to be; it is an inward life, a vital sensibility which contains our manner of feeling what and how we are; it is the state of our desires and tendencies, of inwardly seeing, hearing, tasting, relishing and feeling that which passes within us; it is that to us inwardly with regard to ourselves which our senses of seeing, hearing, feeling, and so forth, are with regard to things that are without or external to us . . .

It is the sensibility of the soul that must receive what this world can communicate to it. It is the sensibility of the soul that must receive what God can communicate to it. Reason may follow after in either case and view through its own glass what is done, but it can do no more.

You have the height and depth of eternity in you

O man! consider yourself. Here you stand in the earnest, perpetual strife of good and evil. All nature is continually at work to bring about the great redemption. The whole creation is travailing in pain and laborious working to be delivered from the vanity of time. And will you be asleep?

Everything you hear or see says nothing, shows nothing to you but what either eternal light or eternal darkness has brought forth; for as day and night divide the whole of our time, so heaven and hell divide the whole of our thoughts, words and actions. Stir which way you will, do or design what you will, you must be an agent with the one or the other.

You cannot stand still because you live in the perpetual workings of temporal and eternal nature; if you work not with the good, the evil that is in nature carries you along with it. You have the height and depth of eternity in you, and therefore, be doing what you will, in either the closet, the field, the shop or the church, you are sowing that which grows and must be reaped in eternity.

A mistaken atonement theology

They who suppose the wrath and anger of God upon fallen man to be a state of mind in God himself, to be a political kind of just indignation, a point of honourable resentment which the sovereign Deity, as Governor of the world, ought not to recede from but must have a sufficient satisfaction done to his offended authority before he can (consistently with his sovereign honour) receive the sinner into his favour, hold the doctrine of the necessity of Christ's atoning life and death in a mistaken sense.

That many good souls may hold this doctrine in this simplicity of belief I make no manner of doubt. But when books are written to impose and require this belief of others as the only saving faith in the life and death of Christ, it is then an error that ceases to be innocent.

For neither reason nor Scripture will allow us to bring wrath into God himself, as a temper of his mind, who is only infinite, unalterable, overflowing love, as unchangeable in love as he is in power and goodness.

Fire from a flint

Salvation is a birth of life, but reason can no more bring forth this birth than it can kindle life in a plant or animal. You might as well write the word flame upon the outside of a flint, and then expect that its imprisoned fire should be kindled by it, as to imagine that any images or ideal speculations of reason painted in your brain should raise your soul out of its state of death and kindle the divine life in it.

No! Would you have fire from a flint, its house of death must be shaken and its chains of darkness broken off by the strokes of a steel upon it. This must of all necessity be done to your soul; its imprisoned fire must be awakened by the sharp strokes of a steel, or no true light of life can arise in it.

A PRAYER

O heavenly Father, touch and penetrate and shake and awaken the inmost depth and centre of my soul, that all that is within me may cry and call to you. Strike the flinty rock of my heart that the water of eternal life may spring up in it. Oh break open the gates of the great deep in my soul, that your light may shine in upon me, that I may enter into your Kingdom of light and love, and in your light see light.

The spirit of prayer alone avails

God, the only good of all intelligent natures, is not an absent or distant God, but is more present in and to our souls than our own bodies.

And we are strangers to heaven and without God in this world for this only reason, because we are void of that spirit of prayer which alone can and never fails to unite us with the one only Good, and to open heaven and the Kingdom within us.

A root set in the finest soil, in the best climate, and blessed with all that sun and rain and air can do for it, is not in so sure a state of its growth to perfection as every man may be whose spirit aspires after all that which God is ready and infinitely desirous to give him.

For the sun meets not the springing bud that stretches towards him with half that certainty as God, the source of all good, communicates himself to the soul that longs to partake of him.

God, the boundless abyss of all that is good

God, considered in himself, is as infinitely separate from all possibility of doing hurt or willing pain to any creature as he is from a possibility of suffering pain or hurt from the hand of man.

This is because he is in himself, in his holy Trinity, nothing else but the boundless abyss of all that is good and sweet and amiable, and therefore stands in the utmost contrariety to everything that it not a blessing – in an eternal impossibility of willing and intending a moment's pain or hurt to any creature.

For from this unbounded source of goodness and perfection nothing but infinite streams of blessing are perpetually flowing forth upon all nature and creatures in a more incessant plenty then rays of light stream from the sun.

And as the sun has but one nature and can give forth nothing but the blessings of light, so the holy triune God has but one nature and intent towards all the creation, which is to pour forth the riches and sweetness of his divine perfections upon everything that is capable of them and according to its capacity to receive them.

God, the fountain of all good

God is the Good, the unchangeable, overflowing fountain of Good that sends forth nothing but Good to all eternity. He is the love itself, the unmixed, unmeasurable love, doing nothing but from love, giving nothing but gifts of love to everything that he has made; requiring nothing of all his creatures but the spirit and fruits of that love which brought them into being.

Oh, how sweet is this contemplation of the height and depth of the riches of divine love! With what attraction must it draw every thoughtful man to return love for love to this overflowing fountain of boundless goodness!

View every part of our redemption, from Adam's first sin to the resurrection of the dead, and you will find nothing but successive mysteries of that first love which created angels and men. All the mysteries of the gospel are only so many marks and proofs of God's desiring to make his love triumph in the removal of sin and disorder from all nature and creatures.

Christ in us the hope of glory

A Christ not in us is the same thing as a Christ not ours. If we are only so far with Christ as to own and receive the history of his birth, person and character, if this is all that we have of him, we are as much without him, as much left to ourselves, as little helped by him as those evil spirits which cried out 'we know thee, who thou art, thou holy one of God'.

It is the language of Scripture that Christ in us is our hope of glory, that Christ formed in us, growing and raising his own life and spirit in us, is our only salvation. For since the serpent, sin, death and hell are all essentially within us, the very growth of our nature, must not our redemption be equally inward, an inward essential death to this state of our souls, and an inward growth of a contrary life within us?

The inward new man

All our salvation consists in the manifestation of
the nature, life and spirit of Jesus Christ in our
inward new man. This alone is Christian redemption, this alone delivers from the guilt and power
of sin, this alone redeems, renews and regains the
first life of God in the soul of man. Everything
besides this is self, is fiction, is propriety, is own
will, and however coloured is only your old man,
with all his deeds.

Enter therefore with all your heart into this truth,
let your eye be always upon it, do everything in
view of it, try everything by the truth of it, love
nothing but for the sake of it. Wherever you go,
whatever you do, at home or abroad, in the field
or at church, do all in a desire of union with
Christ, in imitation of his tempers and inclinations, and look upon all as nothing but that
which exercises and increases the spirit and life of
Christ in your soul.

A prayer

O heavenly Father, infinite, fathomless depth of never-ceasing love, save me from myself, from the disorderly workings of my fallen, long-corrupted nature, and let my eyes see, my heart and spirit feel and find your salvation in Christ Jesus.

O God who made me for yourself, to show forth your goodness in me, manifest, I humbly beseech you, the life-giving power of your holy nature within me; help me to such a true and living faith in you, such strength of hunger and thirst after the birth, life and spirit of your holy Jesus in my soul, that all that is within me may be turned from every inward thought or outward work that is not you, your holy Jesus and heavenly working in my soul.

A true and false desire

Do not all Christians desire to have Christ to be their Saviour? Yes. But here is the deceit; all would have Christ to be their Saviour in the *next* world and to help them into heaven when they die by his power and merits with God.

But this is not willing Christ to be your Saviour; for his salvation, if it is to be had, must be had in *this* world; if he saves you it must be done in this life by changing all that is within you, by helping you to a new heart, as he helped the blind to see, the lame to walk and the dumb to speak.

For to have salvation from Christ is nothing else but to be made like unto him; it is to have his humility and meekness, his mortification and self-denial, his renunciation of the spirit, wisdom and honours of this world, his love of God, his desire of doing God's will and seeking only his honour.

To have these tempers formed and begotten in your heart is to have salvation from Christ. But if you will not to have these tempers brought forth in you, if your faith and desire does not seek and cry to Christ for them in the same reality as the lame asked to walk and the blind to see, then you must be said to be unwilling to have Christ to be your Saviour.

Consider the treasure you have within you

If you have never yet owned him, if you have wandered from him as far as the Prodigal Son from his father's house, yet is he still with you, he is the gift of God to you, and if you will turn to him and ask of him, he has living water for you.

Poor sinner! Consider the treasure you have within you. The Saviour of the world, the eternal Word of God, lies hidden in you, as a spark of the divine nature which is to overcome sin and death and hell within you and generate the life of heaven again in your soul. Turn to your heart and your heart will find its Saviour, its God within itself.

You see, hear and feel nothing of God because you seek for him abroad with your outward eyes, you seek for him in books, in controversies, in the Church and outward exercises, but there you will not find him till you have first found him in your heart. Seek for him in your heart and you will never seek in vain, for there he dwells, there is the seat of his light and his holy spirit.

Inward renewal

When once you are well grounded in this inward worship, you will have learnt to live to God above time and place. For every day will be a Sunday to you, and wherever you go you will have a priest, a church and an altar with you.

When God has all that he should have of your heart, when renouncing the will, judgement, tempers and inclinations of your old man you are wholly given up to the obedience of the light and spirit of God within you, to will only in his will, to love only in his love, to be wise only in his wisdom, then it is that everything you do is as a song of praise, and the common business of your life is a conforming to God's will on earth, as angels do in heaven.

The work of repentance

All depends upon your right submission and obedience to the speaking of God in your soul. Stop therefore all self-activity, listen not to the suggestions of your own reason, run not on in your own will, but be retired, silent, passive and humbly attentive to this new risen light within you.

Open your heart, your eyes and ears, to all its impressions. Let it enlighten, teach, frighten, torment, judge and condemn you as it pleases; turn not away from it, hear all it says, seek for no relief out of it, consult not with flesh and blood but, with a heart full of faith and resignation to God, pray only this prayer, that God's Kingdom may come and his will be done in your soul.

Stand faithfully in this state of preparation, thus given up to the spirit of God, and then the work of your repentance will be wrought in God, and you will soon find that he that is in you is much greater than all that are against you.

Mortifications

As to the nature of our self-denials and mortifications, considered in themselves they have nothing of goodness or holiness, nor are any real parts of our sanctification; they are not the true food or nourishment of the divine life in our souls, they have no quickening, sanctifying power in them.

Their only worth consists in this, that they remove the impediments of holiness, break down that which stands between God and us, and make way for the quickening, sanctifying spirit of God to operate on our souls. Which operation of God is the one only thing that can raise the divine life in the soul, or help it to the smallest degree of real holiness or spiritual life.

All the activity of man in the works of self-denial has no good in itself, but is only to open an entrance for the one only good, the light of God, to operate upon us.

The way of salvation for all men

There is but one salvation for all mankind, and that is the life of God in the soul. God has but one design or intent towards all mankind, and that is to introduce or generate his own life, light and spirit in them, that all may be as so many images, temples and habitations of the holy Trinity.

This is God's will to all Christians, Jews and heathens. They are all equally the desire of his heart.

Now there is but one possible way for man to attain this salvation. There is not one way for a Jew, another for a Christian and a third for a heathen. No; God is one, human nature is one, salvation is one, and the way to it is one; and that is the desire of the soul turned to God.

Suppose this desire to be awakened and fixed upon God, though in souls that never heard either of the law or gospel, and then the new birth of Christ is formed in those who never heard his name. And these are they 'that shall come from the East and the West and sit down with Abraham and Isaac in the Kingdom of God'.

The divine loadstone

 No sooner is the finite desire of the creature in motion towards God, but the infinite desire of God is united with, co-operates with it.

When therefore the first spark of a desire after God arises in your soul, cherish it with all your care, give all your heart into it, it is nothing less than a touch of the divine loadstone that is to draw you out of the vanity of time into the riches of eternity.

Get up therefore and follow it as gladly as the wise men of the East followed the star from heaven that appeared to them. It will do for you as the star did for them, it will lead you to the birth of Jesus, not in a stable at Bethlehem in Judaea, but to the birth of Jesus in the dark centre of your own fallen soul.

False fire

Would you know whence it is that so many false spirits have appeared in the world who have deceived themselves and others with false fire and false light, laying claim to inspirations, illuminations and openings of the divine life, pretending to do wonders under extraordinary calls from God? It is this; they have turned to God without turning from themselves; would be alive in God before they were dead to their own nature; a thing impossible as for a grain of wheat to be alive before it dies.

Now religion in the hands of self or corrupt nature serves only to discover vices of a worse kind than nature left to itself. Hence are all the disorderly passions of religious men, which burn a worse flame than passions only employed about worldly matters: pride, self-exaltation, hatred and persecution, under a cloak of religious zeal, will sanctify actions which nature left to itself, would be ashamed to own.

The original of all evil

Here we see the plain and true original of all evil, without any perplexity or imputation upon God:

– That evil is nothing else but the wrath and fire and darkness of nature broken off from God;

– That the punishment, the pain or the hell of sin is no designedly prepared or arbitrary penalty inflicted by God, but the natural and necessary state of the creature that leaves or turns from God;

– That the will of the creature is the only opener of all evil or good in the creature. The will stands between God and nature; the will totally resigned and given up to God is one spirit with God and God dwells in it; the will turned from God is taken prisoner in the wrath, fire and darkness of nature.

One way, one truth and one life

Give up yourselves to the meek and humble spirit of the holy Jesus, the overcomer of all fire and pride and wrath. This is the one way, the one truth and the one life. There is no other open door into the sheepfold of God. Everything else is the working of the devil in the fallen nature of man.

Humility must sow the seed, or there can be no reaping in heaven. Look not at pride only as an unbecoming temper; nor at humility only as a decent virtue; for the one is death and the other is life; the one is all hell and the other is all heaven.

So much as you have of pride, so much you have of the fallen angel alive in you; so much as you have of true humility, so much you have of the Lamb of God within you. 'Learn of me for I am meek and lowly of heart.' If this lesson is unlearnt, we must be said to have left our Master, as those disciples did who went back and walked no more with him.

At grass with Nebuchadnezzar

Nothing does or can keep God out of the soul but the desire of the heart turned from him. And the reason of it is this: it is because the life of the soul is in itself nothing but a working will; and therefore wherever the will works or goes, there and there only the soul lives, whether it be in God or the creature.

Whatever it desires, that is the fuel of its fire; and as its fuel is, so is the flame of its life. A will given up to earthly goods is at grass with Nebuchadnezzar and has one life with the beasts of the field. Wherever and in whatever the working will chooses to dwell and delight, that becomes the soul's food, its condition, its body, its clothing and habitation.

Is there anything so frightful as this worldly spirit which turns the soul from God, makes it a house of darkness and feeds it with the food of time? On the other hand, what can be so desirable as the spirit of prayer which empties the soul of all its own evil, separates death and darkness from it, leaves self, time and the world, and becomes one life with Christ?

The distress that stands near the gate of life

Nature must become a torment and burden to itself before it can willingly give itself up to that death through which alone it can pass into life. There is no true and real conversion, whether it be from infidelity or any other life of sin, until a man comes to know and feel that nothing less than his whole nature is to be parted with, and yet finds in himself no possibility of doing it.

This is the inability that can bring us at last to say with the apostle, 'When I am weak, then am I strong'. This is the distress that stands near to the Gate of Life; this is the despair by which we lose all our own life, to find a new one in God.

Happy therefore is it for your friend that he is come thus far, that everything is taken from him on which he trusted and found content in himself. In this state one sigh or look, or the least turning of his heart to God for help, would be the beginning of his salvation.

Every man's life is a continual state of prayer

Every man's life is a continual state of prayer; he is no moment free from it, nor can possibly be so.

For all our natural tempers, be they what they will, ambition, covetousness, selfishness, worldly-mindedness, pride, envy, hatred, malice or any other lust whatever, are all of them in reality only so many different kinds and forms of a spirit of prayer which is inseparable from the heart as weight is from the body.

For every natural temper is nothing else but a manifestation of the desire and prayer of the heart, and shows us how it works and wills. And as the heart works and wills, such and no other is its prayer.

If therefore the working desire of the heart is not habitually turned towards God, if this is not our spirit of prayer, we are necessarily in a state of prayer towards something else that carries us from God and brings all kind of evil into us. Pray we must, as sure as our heart is alive; and therefore when the state of our heart is not a spirit of prayer to God, we pray without ceasing to some or other part of the creation.

Nothing is in vain to the humble soul

Nothing is in vain or without profit to the humble soul; like the bee it takes its honey even from bitter herbs. It stands always in a state of divine growth, and everything that falls upon it is like the dew of heaven to it.

Shut up yourself therefore in this form of humility, all good is enclosed in it; it is a water of heaven that turns the fire of the fallen soul into the meekness of the divine life. Let it be as a garment wherewith you are always covered, and the girdle with which you are girt.

Breathe nothing but in and from its spirit; see nothing but with its eyes; hear nothing but with its ears. And then, whether you are in the church or out of the church, hearing the praises of God or receiving wrongs from men and the world, everything will help forward your growth in the life of God.

Turning to God

Turning to God according to the inward feeling, want and motion of your own heart, in love, in trust, in faith of having from him all that you want to have, this turning thus unto God, whether it be with or without words, is the best form of prayer in the world.

Now no man can be ignorant of the state of his own heart or a stranger to those tempers that are alive and stirring in him, and therefore no man can want a form of prayer; for what should be the form of his prayer but that which the condition and state of his heart demands?

For prayers not formed according to the real state of your heart are but like a prayer to be pulled out of a deep well when you are not in it. Hence you may see how unreasonable it is to make a mystery of prayer, or an art that needs so much instruction; since every man is, and only can be, directed by his own inward state and condition when and how and what he is to pray.

Different forms of prayer

Every man that has any feeling of the weight of his sin, or any true desire to be delivered from it by Christ has learning and capacity enough to make his own prayer. For praying is not speaking forth eloquently, but simply, the true desire of the heart.

The most simple souls that have accustomed themselves to speak their own desires and wants to God, in such short but true breathings of their hearts to him, will soon know more of prayer and the mysteries of it than any persons who have only their knowledge from learning and learned books.

It is not silence, or a simple petition, or a great variety of outward expressions that alters the nature of prayer, or makes it good or better, but only and solely the reality, steadiness and continuity of the desire; and therefore whether a man offers this desire to God in the silent longing of the heart, or in simple short petitions, or in a great variety of words is of no consequence. But if you would know what I would call a true and great gift of prayer, and what I most of all wish for myself, it is a good heart that stands continually inclined towards God.

A method of prayer

The best help you can have from a book is to read one full of such truths, instructions and awakening informations as force you to see and know who and what and where you are; that God is your All; and that all is misery but a heart and life devoted to him. This is the best outward prayer book you can have, as it will turn you to an inward book and spirit of prayer in your heart.

When for the sake of this inward prayer you retire at any time of the day, never begin until you know and feel why and wherefore you are going to pray; and let this why and wherefore form and direct everything that comes from you whether it be in thought or word. No good desire can languish when once your heart is in this method of prayer; never beginning to pray until you first see how matters stand with you; asking your heart what it wants and having nothing in your prayers but what the known state of your heart puts you upon demanding, saying or offering unto God.

Thus praying you can never pray in vain.

The breath and life of the triune God

There is in the soul of every man the fire and light and love of God, though lodged in a state of hiddenness, inactivity and death until something or other, human or divine, Moses and the prophets, Christ or his apostles, discover its life within us.

For the soul of every man is the breath and life of the triune God, and as such a partaker of the divine nature; but all this divinity is unfelt because overpowered by the workings of flesh and blood until such time as distress, or grace, or both give flesh and blood a shock, open the long-shut-up eyes, and force a man to find something in himself that sense and reason while at quiet were not aware of.

The way of the returning prodigal

Jacob Behmen absolutely requires his reader to be in the way of the returning prodigal. It is not rules of morality observed or an outward blameless form of life that will do: for pride, vanity, envy, self-love and love of the world can be and often are the heart of such a morality of life. But the state of the lost son is quite another thing.

As soon as he comes to himself and has seeing eyes, he will then, like him, see himself far from home; that he has lost his first paradise, his heavenly Father, and the dignity of his first birth; that he is a poor, beggarly slave in a foreign land, hungry, ragged, and starving among the lowest kind of beasts, not so well fed and clothed as they are.

Wherever the gospel itself is received and professed without something of this preparation of heart, without this sensibility of the lost son, there it can only be a stone of stumbling and help the earthly man to form a religion of notions and opinions from the unfelt meaning of the letter of the gospel.

The one will of love

 As love has no by-ends, wills nothing but its own increase, so everything is as oil to its flame; it must have that which it wills, and cannot be disappointed, because everything naturally helps it to live in its own way, and to bring forth its own work.

The spirit of love does not want to be rewarded, honoured or esteemed; its only desire is to propagate itself, and become the blessing and happiness of everything that wants it. And therefore it meets wrath and evil and hatred and oppositon with the same one will as the light meets the darkness, only to overcome it with all its blessings.

Did you want to avoid the wrath or ill-will, or to gain the favour of any persons, you might easily miss of your ends; but if you have no will but to all goodness, everything you meet, be it what it will, must be forced to be assistant to you. For the wrath of an enemy, the treachery of a friend, and every other evil only help the spirit of love to be more triumphant, to live its own life and find all its own blessings in a higher degree.

The purgatory of the whole creation

This is a certain truth that hell and death, curse and misery, can never cease or be removed from the creation until the will of the creature is again as it came from God, and is only a spirit of love that wills nothing but goodness.

All the whole fallen creation, stand it never so long, must groan and travail in pain, this must be its purgatory until every contrariety to the divine will is entirely taken from every creature.

Which is only saying that all the powers and properties of nature are a misery to themselves, can only work in disquiet and wrath, until the birth of the Son of God brings them under the dominion and power of the spirit of love.

Two states or forms of life

There are, in all the possibility of things, but two states or forms of life. The one is nature and the other is God manifested in nature; and as God and nature are both within you, so you have it in your power to love and work with which you will, but are under a necessity of doing either the one or the other. There is no standing still. Life goes on and is always bringing forth its realities, which way soever it goes.

The properties of nature are, and can be, nothing else in their own life but a restless hunger, disquiet and blind strife for they know not what, until the properties of light and love have got possession of them. Blind nature does all the work, and must be the doer of it, until the Christ of God is born in the natural man.

Goodness is only a sound, and virtue a mere strife of natural passions, until the spirit of love is the breath of everything that lives and moves in the heart. For love is the one only blessing and goodness and God of nature; and you have no true religion, are no worshipper of the one true God, but in and by that spirit of love which is God himself living and working in you.

All are called to be holy

 Though all are not called to be prophets or apostles, yet all are called to be holy, as he who has called them is holy, to be perfect as their heavenly Father is perfect, to be like-minded with Christ, to will only as God wills, to do all to his honour and glory, to renounce the spirit of this world, to have their conversation in heaven, to set their affections on things above, to love God with all their heart, soul and spirit, and their neighbour as themselves.

Behold a work as great, as divine and supernatural as that of a prophet and an apostle.

The natural state of our tempers

The natural state of our tempers has a variety of covers, under which they lie concealed at times, both from ourselves and others; but when this or that accident happens to displace such or such a cover, then that which lay hidden under it breaks forth. And then we vainly think that this or that outward occasion has not shown us how we are within, but has only infused or put into us a wrath, or grief, or envy which is not our natural state, or of our own growth, or has all that it has from our own inward state.

But this is mere blindness and self-deceit, for it is as impossible for the mind to have any grief or wrath or joy but what it has all from its own inward state, as for the instrument to give forth any other harmony or discord but that which is within and from itself.

Persons, things and occurrences may strike our instrument improperly and variously, but as we are in ourselves, such is our outward sound, whatever strikes us. If our inward state is the renewed life of Christ within us, then every thing and occasion, let it be what it will, only makes the same life to sound forth and show itself.

God as a consuming fire

God is said to be a consuming fire. But to whom? To the fallen angels and lost souls. But why and how is he so to them? It is because those creatures have lost all that they had from God but the fire of their nature, and therefore God can only be found and manifested in them as a consuming fire.

Though God be nothing but love, yet they are under the wrath and vengeance of God because they have only that fire in them which is broken off from the light and love of God, and so can know or feel nothing of God but his fire of nature in them. And yet it is still strictly true that there is no wrath in God himself, that he has not changed in his temper towards the creatures, that he does not cease to be one and the same infinite fountain of goodness, infinitely flowing forth in the riches of his love upon all and every life.

God is not changed from love to wrath, but the creatures have changed their own state in nature, and so the God of nature can only be manifested in them according to their own state in nature.

Christ given into us

Christ given for us is neither more nor less than Christ given into us. And he is in no other sense our full, perfect and sufficient atonement than as his nature and spirit are born and formed in us, which so purge us from our sins that we are thereby in him, and by him dwelling in us, become new creatures, having our conversation in heaven.

As Adam is truly our defilement and impurity, by his birth in us, so Christ is our atonement and purification, by our being born again of him, and having thereby quickened and revived in us that first divine life which was extinguished in Adam.

And therefore, as Adam purchased death for us, just so in the same manner, in the same degree, and in the same sense, Christ purchases life for us. And each of them solely by their own inward life in us.

The innocent Christ

The innocent Christ did not suffer to quiet an angry deity, but merely as co-operating, assisting and uniting with that love of God which desired our salvation.

He did not suffer in our place or stead, but only on our account, which is a quite different matter. And to say that he suffered in our place and stead is as absurd, as contrary to Scripture, as to say that he rose from the dead and ascended into heaven in our place and stead, that we might be excused from it.

For his sufferings, death, resurrection and ascension are all of them equally on our account, for our sake, for our good and benefit, but none of them possible to be in our stead.

Election and reprobation

Nothing is elected, foreseen, predestinated or called according to the purpose of God but this seed of the new man, because the one eternal, unchangeable purpose of God towards man is only this, namely that man should be a heavenly image or son of God.

On the other hand nothing is reprobated, rejected or cast out by God but the earthly nature which came from the fall of Adam. This is the only vessel of wrath, the son of perdition that can have no share in the promises and blessings of God.

Here you have the whole unalterable ground of divine election and reprobation; it relates not to any particular number of people or division of mankind, but solely to the two natures that are, both of them, without exception, in every individual of mankind. All that is earthly, serpentine and devilish in every man is reprobated and doomed to destruction; and the heavenly seed of new birth in every man is that which is chosen, ordained and called to eternal life.

Election therefore and reprobation, as respecting salvation, equally relate to every man in the world; because every man, as such, has that in him which *only* is elected, and that in him which *only* is reprobated, namely the earthly nature and the heavenly seed of the Word of God.

Divine love

Divine love is perfect peace and joy, it is a freedom from all disquiet, it is all content and mere happiness and makes everything to rejoice in itself.

Love is the Christ of God. Wherever it comes, it comes as the blessing and happiness of every natural life, as the restorer of every lost perfection, a redeemer from all evil, a fulfiller of all righteousness, and a peace of God which passeth all understanding.

Through all the universe of things nothing is uneasy, unsatisfied or restless but because it is not governed by love, or because its nature has not reached or attained the full birth of the spirit of love. For when that is done every hunger is satisfied, and all complaining, murmuring, accusing, resenting, revenging and striving are as totally suppressed and overcome as the coldness, thickness and horror of darkness are suppressed and overcome by the breaking-forth of the light.

If you ask why the spirit of love cannot be displeased, cannot be disappointed, cannot complain, accuse, resent or murmur, it is because divine love desires nothing but itself, it is its own good, it has all when it has itself, because nothing is good but itself and its own working; for love is God and he that dwells in God dwells in love.

Covetousness, envy, pride and wrath

Covetousness, envy, pride and wrath are the four elements of self, or nature, or hell, all of them inseparable from it.

Now covetousness, pride and envy are not three different things, but only three different names for the restless workings of one and the same will or desire which, as it differently torments itself, takes these different names.

And therefore, when fallen from God, this desire's three first births, which are quite inseparable from it, are covetousness, envy and pride.

It must covet because it is a desire proceeding from want; it must envy because it is a desire turned to self; it must assume and arrogate because it is a desire founded on a real want of exaltation or a higher state.

Now wrath, which is a fourth birth from these three, can have no existence until some or all of these three are *contradicted*, or have something done to them that is contrary to their will; and then it is that wrath is necessarily born, and not until then.

Resentment

To rejoice in a resentment gratfied appears now to me to be quite frightful. For what is it in reality but rejoicing that my own serpent of self has new life and strength given to it, and that the precious Lamb of God is denied entrance to my soul?

For this is the strict truth of the matter. To give in to resentment and go willingly to gratify it is calling up the courage of your own serpent and truly helping it to be more stout and valiant and successful in you.

On the other hand, to give up resentment of every kind and on every occasion, however artfully, beautifully, outwardly coloured, and to sink down into the humility of meekness under all contrariety, contradiction and injustice, always turning the other cheek to the smiter, however haughty, is the best of all prayers, the surest of all means to have nothing but Christ living and working in you, as the Lamb of God that takes away every sin that ever had power over your soul.

The inward strong man of pride

The inward strong man of pride, the diabolical self, has his higher works within; he dwells in the strength of the heart, and has every power and faculty of the soul offering continual incense to him.

His memory, his will, his understanding, his imagination are always at work for him and for no one else. His memory is the faithful repository of all the fine things that self has ever done; and lest anything of them should be lost or forgotten, she is continually setting them before his eyes. His will, though it has all the world before it, yet goes after nothing but as self sends it. His understanding is ever upon the stretch for new projects to enlarge the dominions of self; and if this fails, imagination comes in as the last and truest support of self; she makes him a king and mighty lord of castles in the air.

This is that full-born natural self that must be pulled out of the heart and totally denied, or there can be no disciple of Christ; which is only saying this plain truth, that the apostate, self-idolatrous nature of the old man must be put off, or there can be no new creature in Christ.

The multiplicity of wills

'Thy Kingdom come, thy will be done' is the one will and one hunger that feeds the soul with the life-giving bread of heaven. This will is always fulfilled, it cannot possibly be sent empty away, for God's Kingdom must manifest itself with all its riches in that soul which wills nothing else.

If you have no inward peace, if religious comfort is still wanting, it is because you have more wills than one. For the multiplicity of wills is the very essence of fallen nature, and all its evil, misery and separation from God lies in it; and as soon as you return to and allow only this one will, you are returned to God, and must find the blessedness of his Kingdom within you.

Nothing can put an end to this multiplicity of wills in fallen man which is his death to God, nothing can be the resurrection of the divine nature within him, which is his only salvation, but the cross of Christ – not that wooden cross on which he was crucified, but that cross on which he was crucified through the whole course of his life in the flesh. It is our fellowship with him on this cross through the whole course of our lives that is our union with him.

Your heart as a den of thieves

You will perhaps say it is your very heart that keeps you a stranger to Christ and him to you, because your heart is all bad, as unholy as a den of thieves.

I answer that the finding this to be the state of your heart is the real finding of Christ in it. For nothing else but Christ can reveal and make manifest the sin and evil in you. And he that discovers is the same Christ that takes away sin. So that as soon as complaining guilt sets itself before you and will be seen, you may be assured that Christ is in you of a truth.

Christ must first come as a discoverer and reprover of sin. It is the infallible proof of his holy presence within you. Hear him, reverence him, submit to him as a discoverer and reprover of sin.

Own his power and his presence in the feeling of your guilt and then he that wounded will heal, he that found out the sin will take it away, and he that showed you your den of thieves will turn it into a holy temple of Father, Son and Holy Ghost.

The spirit of prayer is for all times

The poverty of our fallen nature, the depraved workings of flesh and blood, the corrupt tempers of our polluted birth in this world do us no hurt so long as the spirit of prayer works contrary to them and longs for the first birth of the light and spirit of heaven.

All our natural evil ceases to be our own evil as soon as our will-spirit turns from it. It then changes its nature, loses all its poison and death, and only becomes our holy cross on which we happily die from self and this world into the kingdom of heaven.

Reading is good, hearing is good, conversation and meditation are good; but they are only good at times and occasions.

But the spirit of prayer is for all times and all occasions. It is a lamp that is to be always burning, a light to be ever shining; everything calls for it, everything is to be done in it and governed by it, because it is and means and wills nothing else but the whole totality of the soul not doing this or that, but wholly, incessantly given up to God to be where and what and how he pleases.

Inward and outward religion

He that thinks or holds that outward exercises of religion hurt or are too low for his degree of spirituality shows plainly that his spirituality is only in idea.

The truly spiritual man is he that sees God in all things and all things in God. Every outward thing has the nature of a sacrament to him.

To such a one the outward institutions of religion are ten times more dear and valuable than to those that are less spiritual. As the truly charitable man loves to meet outward objects of charity, as the truly humble man loves to meet outward occasions of being abased, so the truly spiritual man loves all outward objects and institutions that can exercise the religion of the heart.

And to think that the spirituality of religion is hurt by the observance of outward institutions of religion is as absurd as to think that the inward spirit of charity is hurt by the observance of outward acts of charity, or the spiritual joy of the heart destroyed by singing an outward hymn, as our Saviour and his apostles did.

Speech and silence

The spiritual life is nothing else but the working of the spirit of God within us, and therefore our own silence must be a great part of our preparation for it, and much speaking or delight in it will be often no small hindrance of that good which we can only have from hearing what the spirit and voice of God speaks within us.

This is not enough known by religious persons; they rejoice in kindling a fire of their own, and delight too much in hearing of their own voice and so lose that inward unction from above which can alone newly create their hearts.

To speak with the tongues of men or angels on religious matters is a much less thing than to know how to stay the mind upon God, and abide with him in the closet of our hearts, observing, loving, adoring and obeying his holy power within us.

I have written very largely on the spiritual life, and he understands not my writings, nor the end of them, who does not see that their whole drift is to call all Christians to a God and Christ within them as the only possible life, light and power of all goodness they can ever have. I invite all people to the marriage of the Lamb, but no one to myself.

Sources

Only one of Law's later writings appears to be currently in print, namely *The Spirit of Love*, published in one volume with *A Serious Call to a Devout and Holy Life* by SPCK in the Western Classics of Spirituality series. *The Spirit of Love* was also reprinted in 1969 in one volume with *The Spirit of Prayer* edited by Sidney Spencer and published by James Clarke. The standard edition of Law's works was published in nine volumes by G. Moreton, London 1892. Alexander Whyte's anthology of 1893, *Characters and Characteristics of William Law, Non-Juror and Mystic*, Hodder and Stoughton 1893, contains extracts of varying length arranged by subject. Stephen Hobhouse's *Selected Mystical Writings of William Law*, Rockliff 1938, revised edition 1948, consists of much fewer and much longer extracts from all the more important mystical writings, together with useful notes and comments. Hobhouse's book was reprinted a number of times and may be relatively easy to find; Whyte's, unfortunately, is a rarity. There is a useful short bibliography in Henri Talon's *William Law: A Study in Literary Craftsmanship*, Rockliff 1948, another good book unfortunately out of print.

For this selection of readings arranged for devotional purposes a few minor omissions and adjustments have been made to the original text. Capitals and italics are much more sparingly used than in the original. Law is not entirely consistent in his use of *thee, thou* and *you*, and for the purposes of this book the modern form has been adopted throughout.

Index

AA   An Appeal to All who Doubt
CR   The Ground and Reasons of Christian
         Regeneration
D   A Demonstration of the Gross and
         Fundamental Errors of a Late Book
L   A Collection of Letters
Ms   An unpublished manuscript quoted by
         Hobhouse
SL   The Spirit of Love
SP   The Spirit of Prayer
T   An Earnest and Serious Answer to Dr Trapp
         Some Animadversions upon Dr Trapp's
         Late Reply
WDK   The Way to Divine Knowledge